The One and ONLY You

WRITTEN BY: ANNA THOMPSON

ILLUSTRATED BY: DARE HARCOURT

WestBow Press books may be ordered through booksellers or by contacting:

WestBow Press
A Division of Thomas Nelson & Zondervan
1663 Liberty Drive
Bloomington, IN 47403
www.westbowpress.com
844-714-3454

Interior Image Credit: Dare Hardcourt

ISBN: 979-8-3850-0655-7 (sc)
ISBN: 979-8-3850-0656-4 (hc)
ISBN: 979-8-3850-0657-1 (e)

Library of Congress Control Number: 2023916747

Print information available on the last page.

WestBow Press rev. date: 10/4/2023

WESTBOW
PRESS®
A DIVISION OF THOMAS NELSON
& ZONDERVAN

Dedication

For Emma Jane, our one and only YOU! And for the
peanut we lost too soon, who forever changed us.
This book is a love letter to first and only children
everywhere, for the worrying hearts of parents who fear
stereotypes of "only children," parents who struggle
with secondary infertility or child loss. These journeys
are heartbreaking, isolating, and rarely brought
into the open. May these words help you articulate
that your "only" baby has always been enough.

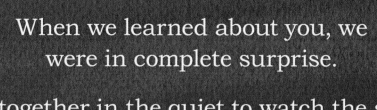

When we learned about you, we
were in complete surprise.

We sat together in the quiet to watch the sunrise.

As we rubbed the sleep from our eyes,
we thought, *Can it be true?*

Then we smiled and prayed for the one and only *you.*

2

You'd already changed us, in more ways than one.

Imagining our life with you, little one, has been such fun.

We counted down 'till you would arrive,
our feisty girl with big brown eyes.

Once you were here, it felt like a dream—the instant way we loved you was more than extreme.

With each new milestone and memory made, your confidence grew, and your hesitation fade.

Our hearts were so full that we wanted even more—
more joy, *more* memories, *more* chapters in store.

So we set about prepping to add to our home,
expecting with certainty the wondrous day to come.

But then something happened, which made us all sad.
We'd bet it all on a dream Mommy had. We'd been
through so much, we thought we were close.
But just like *that*, the door seemed to close.

The reality was different than we had all dreamed,
and giving you a sibling was not as it seemed.

Through prayers, and community, with family and friends, we picked up the pieces and began smiling again.

The truth, little one? You've *always* been enough. Your spirit, your smile, and your character—*so* tough!

YOU CAN DO IT!
YAY!
RUN!
#1!
GO!
GO!
KEEP GOING!
YOU GOT THIS!
LET'S
WE LOVE YOU!
#1 PAPA

We felt like we'd failed you, that you'd
be incomplete. But with time we
learned, it's all so perfectly sweet.

You have people around you,
cheering you on, and your
excellent life is just at its dawn.

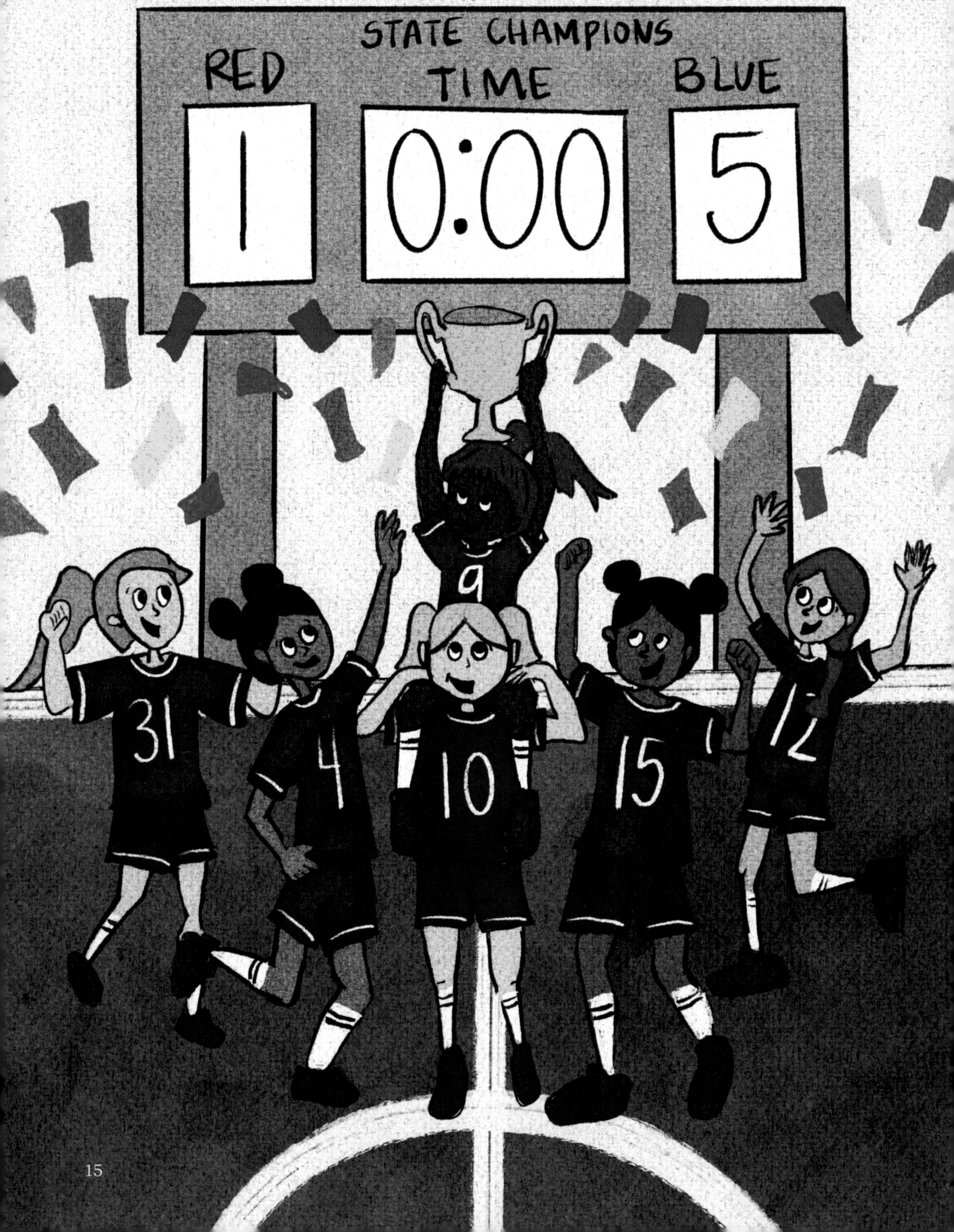
STATE CHAMPIONS
RED
TIME
BLUE
1
0:00
5
31
4
9
10
15
12

You're a true miracle,
a gift from God above.
So never forget just how
much you are loved!

Just because it looks
different, doesn't mean
that it's bad. Trusting God
through your struggles
is not just a fad.

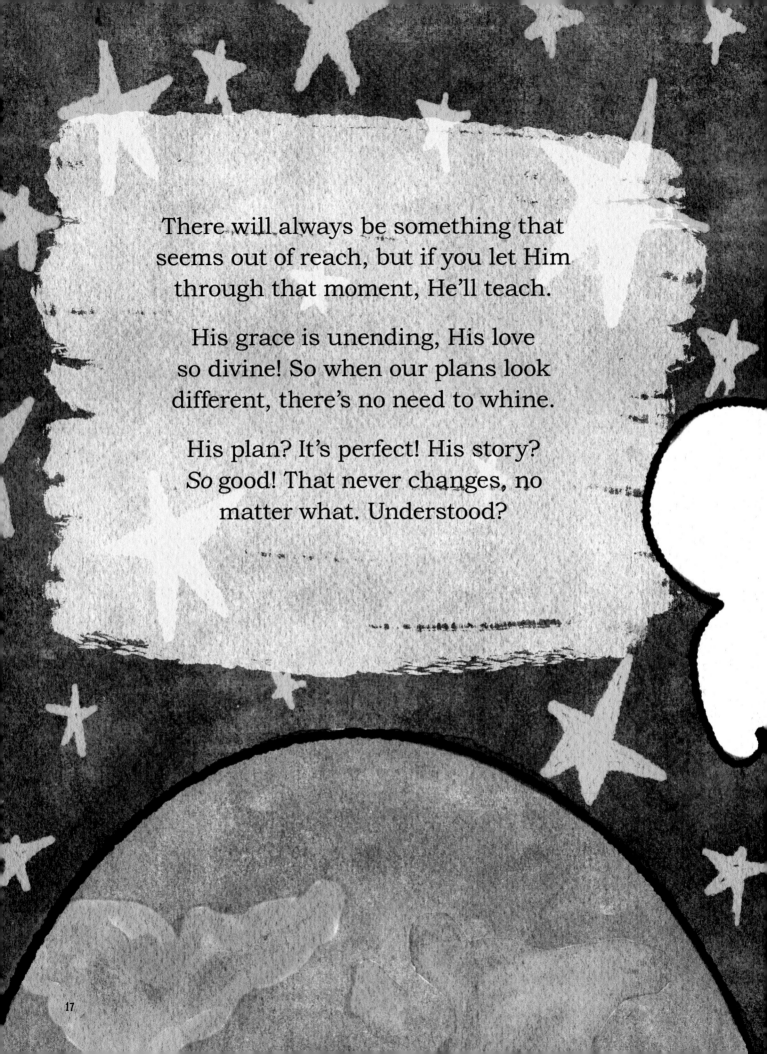

There will always be something that seems out of reach, but if you let Him through that moment, He'll teach.

His grace is unending, His love so divine! So when our plans look different, there's no need to whine.

His plan? It's perfect! His story? *So* good! That never changes, no matter what. Understood?

As you look to the future and dream
your own dreams, we hope your
light for Him continues to beam.

Big things are in store, we
know that much is true.
And we will always be
grateful God gave us the
one and only YOU!

Activities and Questions for families:

Talk about it:

1. Why are different families made up of different people?
2. What types of things do you notice about our family that make us special or unique?
3. What do you love most about our family?
4. Do you ever wish our family was different? If so, how?
5. How do you feel about being an "only child"?
6. Do you agree that God loves us? Do you think that means we should get everything we want?
7. How do you feel when things don't go your way or you don't get what you wanted so badly?
8. Do you think that being happy comes from getting everything you want?
9. (For older children) What do you think is the difference between "joy" and "happiness"?
10. (For older children) Where does "joy" come from?

Activities:

1. Consciously work to be thoughtful of wording in conversations. Language matters in framing experiences, and many common questions and statements can be triggering for those experiencing loss. While the intent is kind, the impact can be hurtful.

2. Go on "adventures" as a family. It can be as simple as a bike ride, a grocery-run, or going to a local park. Framing daily activities as "adventures" helps create positivity and excitement, making every single day memorable.

3. Create a fun family name for your unit, like "The Three Musketeers" or "Team Thompson."

About the author: Anna Thompson is a wife, mother, and communications professional residing in her hometown of Memphis, Tennessee. She is a graduate of Samford University with a BA in Journalism and Mass Communications and minor in Cultural Studies. In 2020, Anna experienced an ectopic pregnancy resulting in the inability for her to naturally conceive more children. Throughout this grief journey, failed IVF procedures, and ultimately the decision to cease fertility treatments, her Christian faith was central to her healing. By sharing her story, it is her hope that others will find comfort, support, and a peace that surpasses all understanding. When she's not working or writing, Anna is passionate about honoring seniors through Forever Young Senior Veterans and spending time with her family and friends.

About the illustrator: Dare Harcourt is a full time artist living and working in Memphis, Tennessee. She attended Ole Miss and graduated with a BS in Communicative Sciences and Disorders. After graduation, she went through some serious health issues. During this time, she began to paint as a way to work through those issues. She fell in love with painting with her first stroke, and her passion for art started from a place of healing and blossomed into a love that continues to bring her immense joy. After realizing her passion for art, she decided to go back to school and received her Masters in Art Education at Memphis College of Art. Each piece of her art is filled with love, hope, and brings a peaceful feeling that she hopes translates to the viewer. When she's not working, you can find her with her black lab, Finn. Finn's vibrant personality provides a lot of inspiration for Dare, and she often jokes of him being her muse.

Printed in the United States
by Baker & Taylor Publisher Services